Communication
Tools for Technicians

Wade King
North Dakota State College of Science

Kendall Hunt
publishing company

Cover image © Shutterstock, Inc.

Kendall Hunt
publishing company

www.kendallhunt.com
Send all inquiries to:
4050 Westmark Drive
Dubuque, IA 52004-1840

Copyright © 2016 by Wade King
ISBN 978-1-4652-9990-1

Kendall Hunt Publishing Company has the exclusive rights to reproduce this work, to prepare derivative works from this work, to publicly distribute this work, to publicly perform this work and to publicly display this work.

All rights reserved. No part of this publication may be reproduced, stored in a retrieval system, or transmitted, in any form or by any means, electronic, mechanical, photocopying, recording, or otherwise, without the prior written permission of the copyright owner.

Printed in the United States of America

TABLE OF CONTENTS

Chapter 1	How Does Technical Communication Work?	1
	What is Technical Communication?	1
	How is Communication at Work Different?	2
	⚙ TOOLBOX: Make Your Points Pointier!	2
	How Does Communication at Work Function?	3
Chapter 2	Short Forms of Communication	5
	Texting and Messaging	6
	Voicemail and Quick Verbal Communications	7
	E-mails and Memos	8
	E-mails and Memos to Coworkers	9
	E-mails and Memos to Other Professionals	10
	Business Letters	11
	⚙ TOOLBOX: Mend It Before You Send It!	13
Chapter 3	The Employment Process	15
	Cover Letters	16
	Resumes	19
	⚙ TOOLBOX: Rules for Resumes	21
	Interviews	22
	⚙ TOOLBOX: General Rules for Interviewing	22
	Follow-up Communication	24

Chapter 4	Technical Description and Instruction		27
	Visual Support		27
	⚙ **TOOLBOX:** Inserting Visuals into Your Document		28
	Technical Description and the Visual Sense		28
	Writing a Technical Description		30
	Example: Front-Drag Spinning Reel		31
	Instruction		34
	Supplemental Information in Instruction		35
	Example: How to Prepare and Rig a New Fishing Kayak		36
Chapter 5	Reporting Information		43
	Summarizing Information		43
	⚙ **TOOLBOX:** The Past, Present, Future Method		45
	Informal Reports		46
	Formal Reports		47
Chapter 6	Oral Communication		59
	Informal Presentations to Coworkers		59
	⚙ **TOOLBOX:** Talking to the Team—Common Problems in Oral Communication		60
	Formal Presentations		60
	Strategies to Engage Your Audience		61
	Guidelines for Using Digital Presentation Methods		61
	A final Note		62

CHAPTER 1
HOW DOES TECHNICAL COMMUNICATION WORK?

This text has two aims: to provide you with the knowledge necessary to communicate at work and to provide you with practical patterns of communication that work across multiple purposes and modes of communication. In other words, this text is an attempt at filling your toolbox with the tools necessary to get the job done.

WHAT IS TECHNICAL COMMUNICATION?

The most practical definition we have found for technical communication is that it "conveys specific information about a technical subject to a specific audience for a specific purpose" (Michael H. Markel, Director of Technical Communication at Boise State University).

This definition gives us a big picture of communication on the job. Specific *information* might be the specifications a coworker needs for machining a part or the details your boss needs to know about a crash involving the company truck. The specific *audience* is whoever we want to understand the message we are conveying. The specific *purpose* is why we are communicating.

Obviously, the specific information involved with communication at work is critical. Accuracy, clarity, and completeness in presenting information are vital to the process of productivity in a company or organization.

Beyond the information being communicated, audience and purpose are the two most important factors in making sure that a message is understood. Reaching the audience means understanding the audience, even if that takes some homework. An *internal audience* usually involves coworkers with whom you are very familiar. An *external audience* involves communicating with individuals or groups outside of your company, such as suppliers or customers.

Especially when communicating with external audiences, some work may have to be done to understand the audience and their needs and expectations as communicators. For instance, you might approach the manager of a trusted supply company outside your own with a more formal method of communication than if you were simply asking a question of a coworker you see every day. In companies or organizations that require dealing with customers, your communication with a customer is likely going to require more care and an understanding of how you project your company's image than the comfortable internal communication that happens among coworkers.

Purpose may seem simple, since it is simply the reason we are communicating. However, it requires more attention at times because some methods of communication work better than others for a given purpose. For instance, asking your boss for a raise and giving a coworker verification that a project is complete are both internal communications, but the approach and the medium for communicating will be very different. You may want to ask your boss for a raise in a private meeting in his office, while a quick verbal conversation or e-mail would serve the purpose of telling a coworker you have completed a project. The patterns of communication described in this text will give you a number of versatile ways to communicate with others, but making the choice based on the purpose is up to you.

If we have clarity as communicators about all of these components, then we will have more clarity in our overall communication. Managing the specific information we communicate to the audience and using appropriate methods for the purpose are the basic components of good communication.

HOW IS COMMUNICATION AT WORK DIFFERENT?

The factors that make technical communication different from more casual communication or even the writing involved in a composition class are the levels of efficiency and precision involved in creating the language. Technical writing is pointed, precise, and concise, while relaying the message in the most efficient way possible. For the most part, there is no small talk, creating suspense, using flowery language, or trying to appear intelligent by writing paragraph after paragraph to reach a certain length.

As you prepare yourself to communicate on the job, keep in mind that our usual forms of communication are very different from the kind of communication that work requires. Throughout most of

> **TOOLBOX: Make your points pointier!**
>
> The first lesson of this text, then, is to make your points *pointier*. That is a simple way of saying that each written communication at work can generally follow this pattern:
>
> 1. Make a statement at the beginning that *specifically* identifies the main thing the receiver needs to know. (Generally, this should be done as a first paragraph of one or two sentences separate from the rest of the text if you are communicating in a written format).
> 2. In a following paragraph or paragraphs, explain or give more details about that simple introductory statement of purpose.
> 3. Finally, a conclusion will typically call for some sort of action from the receiver of your message, make a recommendation, or sum things up.
>
> This method of communication is similar to sharpening a pencil. When it's sharp, the lines are more clear and defined. When it's dull, the lines are less precise and blurred.

human history, our default mode of communication is telling stories. Stories have the essential pattern of a beginning, middle, and ending. Usually they are told in chronological order. You will see later in this text that chronological order can be very useful in technical communication, but most of technical communication relies on first *making your point*, not starting at the beginning of a story.

Here's an example: let's say that you just wrecked your dad's car. Typically, you would communicate about such an event verbally. Imagine yourself in that situation. It is very unlikely that you would start off the conversation with "Hey Dad, I just wrecked the car. We're going to need to call the insurance company."

Although that is the practical nuts-and-bolts of the situation, you would be more likely to start off with something like: "Hey Dad, you know that intersection down on Main Avenue that's a little bit tricky..." In that communication situation, you don't really want to get to the point because you know how your father is going to respond negatively, so you start at the beginning. At work, though, it's all about getting to the point and being clear with your communication.

Sometimes, people think that it's more polite to start off with small talk. In casual conversation, that is not a problem. When "time is money" and we are working to complete tasks, however, we probably need to find a more efficient way to communicate, especially when it is in writing.

HOW DOES COMMUNICATION AT WORK FUNCTION?

Finally, in this chapter, we would like to present one more vital concept to understanding communication at work. It is useful to look at communication as a message that is sent between a sender and a receiver. This is a very simplistic look at communication, but it reveals an essential component.

Let's take a look at the way we usually view communication:

```
                MESSAGE
SENDER  ─────────────────▶  RECEIVER
```

Quite often, we look at communication as something that we tell someone. In terms of tasks, think of how many times in the past at home or work that you have said something like, "I TOLD [insert name] to clean up, and [he or she] didn't do it!" We are indignant because it seems our message was ignored. But did it get through? What if I yelled something up the stairs to someone behind a closed door with a radio playing? What if I left a message for someone with another person and they didn't pass the message along?

The flaw that is revealed when we look at communication as a one-way street is that *feedback* is missing. If we add feedback to the diagram, it looks like this:

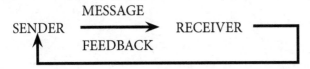

If we look at this in a similar way to the function of electricity, by adding feedback we are completing the circuit. The feedback tells us that the message was indeed received and understood by the person(s) to whom we are sending our communication. As this text progresses, we will see that all four of these areas matter in how we craft our communication. How we send messages makes a difference, the method we choose to carry the message makes a difference, the receiver's ability to understand the message makes a difference, and whether or not there is feedback makes a difference.

In many problems with communication in the workplace, the culprit is inadequate feedback, which relies on both the sender providing the opportunity for feedback and the receiver giving feedback. That makes communication more than just a one-way street.

Beyond this chapter, the text focuses on patterns for communication. Please keep in mind that no matter what kind of communication is happening or what pattern we are using, the best communicators

1. sharpen the points of their communication and
2. work feedback into the loop.

CHAPTER 2
SHORT FORMS OF COMMUNICATION

Probably the most natural form of communication for human beings is telling a story. Think about the way you usually communicate for a moment. You are standing on the sidewalk outside of work and a friend comes by. The content of many of those conversations centers around issues such as "What did you do last night?" or "Let me tell you about what happened to me today…" We share stories. We respond to stories.

Next, think about most of your communication at any job you've had. Beyond the small talk, most communication at work is related to getting the job done. When we are communicating this mission-specific information, we are often tempted to communicate the same way we do informally. However, that is not the most efficient way to communicate.

At work, if we are to communicate most clearly and efficiently, the way to begin our communication is by getting the basic message across immediately. Although this may seem a little bit blunt or direct, getting our main idea or message across first is more important than starting at the "beginning."

Let's examine a scenario: you wreck the company truck and you need to tell your boss about it. This may be similar to a situation many teenagers deal with (and one we described in Chapter 1): you wreck your parents' car and you need to tell them about it.

As we previously discussed, in the personal, informal scenario of telling your parents about an accident, your first statement is not always a blunt "Hey dad, guess what? I wrecked the car." It is much more likely to be a conversation that starts at the beginning of the story. Perhaps you begin with a statement such as "You know that tricky intersection down by the convenience store? Well, I was driving along . . ."

Contrast the scenario with your parents with relaying the news of a wreck to your boss. How would you do it differently? It's probably a good bet that you would not tell as long of a story to your boss, for fear that he or she might get impatient with you because he or she is busy and doesn't have time for a story that may or may not be leading anywhere. Therefore, it is probably better to start the account of what happened for your boss with something more matter-of-fact, such as "I wrecked the company truck this morning on my way back from picking up parts." This might be followed up by more information that clarifies important questions, such as "Everyone was OK, and the police have a report on file. We'll need to find another vehicle for parts pickups while we're working with the insurance on replacing the wrecked vehicle."

The events are still described in the communication to your boss, but there is a more direct message that gets to the point, explains the logistical details, and perhaps looks to the future.

6   Communication: Tools for Technicians

The following pattern is a good one to follow with both verbal and written communications when the message is relatively short:

> **Point**—What is the most important thing you need to tell them?
>
> **Details**—What are the details related to your message?
>
> **Plan**—What are you going to do or what do you expect of your audience?
>
> We call this the PDP method of communication. If we put this into a chart that covers a variety of scenarios, it could be expanded to look like this:
>
> **Point**
>
> Directly address the main idea. If you are communicating via phone or voicemail, identify the purpose of your call. If you are communicating in writing, identify the most important message or question you have for your audience. What do they need to know right up front? NOTE: you should present this idea in a very visual way by writing a short paragraph (a sentence or two) as an introduction to your document.
>
> **Details**
>
> If it is appropriate, this is where you tell your story from the beginning. This is the body of a written document. In the case of our previous scenario, this would be the detailed story of what happened to the company truck, what damage was done, and so on. In the case of other scenarios, you might be providing details of a problem you are experiencing that needs to be solved, outlining a procedure, giving reasons for a new policy, or just explaining your main idea in more detail.
>
> **Plan**
>
> In short communication, your conclusion should look ahead to what needs to be done, perhaps requesting action or asking for some kind of feedback. It is very important to work on the feedback loop, as discussed in Chapter 1. If you are leaving a voicemail, a good closing would be to provide your number and ask the recipient to call you. Here, it helps to think about what kind of a response you want from your audience and be specific.

TEXTING AND MESSAGING

With very short communication, such as texting and instant messaging technologies, it is important to remember that the communication can't leave out essential parts of the message. One of the most difficult communication tasks can be trying to put a message into a very short format while still following the basic PDP flow. Keep in mind that some messages probably shouldn't use this extremely short, quick format. If you're asking your boss for a raise and you want to make a good argument based on sound reasons, you probably need to set an appointment and have a longer conversation. On the other hand, if you need information quickly from someone or need to tell him or her something simple, a quick text message might be the ticket.

Let's look at another scenario: You need to ask a coworker to provide you with a specification, such as the proper grease for a fitting on a machine. You need the information right away, since you're trying to complete a project by the end of the day. The coworker who knows the information is not currently in the shop, but you all carry mobile phones.

It may be tempting to try to communicate in an ultra-quick format, such as simply texting: "What kind of grease does the tailstock fitting on the lathe take?" but keep in mind that you haven't indicated any kind of urgency, so your audience doesn't know why or when you need the information.

A good method following PDP would be the following:

> "What kind of grease does the tailstock fitting on the lathe take? I need to finish this project by 5:00 pm. Please let me know ASAP."

Note how the first question forms the **point**, the urgency of needing to finish by 5:00 pm forms the **details**, and the request for information forms the **plan** (or feedback that you need).

It may take a little bit of extra time to text the additional information beyond the initial question, but it relays the urgency and asks the audience to act on your request. In cases where time is important, specific deadlines motivate people.

VOICEMAIL AND QUICK VERBAL COMMUNICATIONS

Leaving voicemails or quickly getting a message across to someone you are passing in the hallway can also be difficult, since time is very limited. However, once again the PDP method can be utilized in a very rapid-fire manner. As with texting or messaging, a quick voicemail is not the best way to communicate messages with a lot of details, but it can be very effective in the case of a much focused message.

Consider this scenario: you have discussed a problem with shipping with one of your coworkers in the past. You have meant to deal with it several times, but you want to finally solve the issue so you can forget about it. You decide to call the coworker, but you get his voicemail.

Again, it may be tempting to simply leave a message that says "Call me when you get a chance," but that might not result in the coworker seeing that communication as a priority.

Using PDP, a good voicemail for this scenario might be:

"Bob, I'm calling to set a meeting with you regarding the shipping issue we discussed. Please call me back at extension 2103."

This might not seem like a very complete message at first glance, but remember it is just a preview of a much larger discussion. The PDP elements are all there: **Point:** you want to set a meeting;

8 Communication: Tools for Technicians

Details: the meeting is about the shipping issue you've discussed in the past; and **Plan:** you would like him to call you back to talk about it further.

E-MAILS AND MEMOS

Format for e-mails and memos is very simple. The memorandum began as a short note, usually used to communicate messages within a company. Although the format has changed over the decades, it has been standardized to a heading with several elements that most importantly identify the sender and receiver, as well as a body section that contains the message. It is easy to see how e-mail was developed using the same elements.

A typical e-mail or memo format, illustrating the PDP method of short communication, appears below:

To: [name of receiver]
CC: [optional, see explanation below]
From: [your name]
Subject: [a short description of the topic]
Date: [month, day, and year]

One- or two-sentence introduction that distills the message down to its main **point**.

A paragraph (or more) offering **details** or explanation of the main point.

A final paragraph that identifies the **plan** or outcome. The final sentence should encourage feedback where appropriate.

Another aspect that can be added to the memo is the CC: line or BCC: line. CC stands for Carbon Copy and BCC stands for Blind Carbon Copy. CC: is used in both memos and e-mails when you are emphasizing that you are sharing the information with someone else. You might use CC: to keep someone "in the loop" of communication, when they are not the primary recipient. BCC: is used for the same purpose, mostly in e-mail, when you do not want the recipient to know you are sharing the message with the person identified. Both of the designations were developed in a time when copies of a memo were made by rolling a sheet of carbon paper in between two sheets of paper in the typewriter in order to produce an instant copy of the document.

Finally, the subject line in a memo can also be labeled as "Re:," which is short for "regarding." E-mail software often uses this tag instead of "Subject."

The next two sections deal with e-mails and memos directed to two different audiences: coworkers (internal audiences) and other professionals you might be contacting (external audiences). The reason for separating the two is that coworkers are general people with whom you are familiar and require a lower level of formality than when you are communicating with, for instance, a professional who works for another company and perhaps someone who you have never met.

E-MAILS AND MEMOS TO COWORKERS

Writing an e-mail or a memo to someone you already work with requires less formality than writing to someone you don't know. Below is a pretty typical memo to a coworker:

EXAMPLE

> To: Bob Jones
> From: David Ramsey
> Subject: Drill press replacement
> Date: September 22, 2015
>
> In looking over my records, I saw that the drill press in your area is due for replacement, but I need to clarify a couple of issues before we order a new one:
>
> 1. What kind of vise will we need to install on the drill press?
> 2. Does the current drill press have enough torque for driving the bits we are currently using, or do we need to upgrade to a more powerful one?
>
> Please let me know by next Monday, and I'll put an order in with our tool supplier.

Note that the previous memo is short and to the point. The details provided after the main point is established consist of two simple questions. The plan, or closing, identifies the next step.

Below is another example, but this time it contains a bit more formality, since it is a memo from a supervisor to an entire work team. It also clarifies a company policy that involves compliance with government standards.

EXAMPLE

> To: Shop Floor Employees
> From: David Ramsey, Production Supervisor
> Subject: Safety
> Date: October 30, 2015
>
> Please remember to wear safety glasses in all areas of the shop marked with yellow safety tape on the floor. This is a company policy and a condition of employment.
>
> Recently, there have been several incidents reported of near-miss eye injuries. In addition, I have observed that some employees have not been wearing safety glasses when operating machinery. Due to OSHA regulations and our own concern for your safety, please follow all safety policies. Please be aware that failure to comply with safety policies will reflect on your performance ratings.
>
> If you have any questions about these policies, or to request a pair of safety glasses, please contact me in my office or at extension 222.

E-MAILS AND MEMOS TO OTHER PROFESSIONALS

In some instances, especially involving the use of e-mail, we may need to send a short message or request to someone who is a stranger to us. In that instance, we also increase our level of formality while maintaining the same efficient PDP structure.

Below is an example of an e-mail written to request information from a parts supplier.

EXAMPLE

> To: jeff.miller@partssupplyofomaha.net
> From: daveramsey@machineexperts.com
> Subject: Information request
> Date: November 4, 2015
>
> Jeff:
>
> I would like to request a list of the various sizes of tooling caddy boxes that your company has in stock.
>
> As a production supervisor at Machine Experts, I often work with employees needing to change multiple tools throughout the day on their machines. Your line of machine caddies looks like it could provide us with more efficiency and safer tool storage, but I want to make sure that there are sizes that are available for our needs before ordering.
>
> I would prefer a response by November 20 so that I can finish my supply ordering for the month.
>
> Thank you for considering my request,
>
> David Ramsey
>
> Production Supervisor
>
> Machine Experts, Inc.
>
> daveramsey@machineexperts.com

Note that in the previous example, some elements similar to a business letter have been added to increase the formality of addressing someone we have never met. We use a greeting that addresses the person by name with a colon after it, an element you will see in the section coming up on business letters. In addition, we add a formal closing and identify ourselves with an e-mail signature.

Finally, note that once again, we have used the PDP method with a short introduction that identifies the main point, a middle section that adds details, and a closing that identifies the plan or specific request.

BUSINESS LETTERS

Due to the common usage of e-mail in business and industry, the formal business letter has become used less often. For most information requests and replies, e-mail is the preferred method. In addition, the internet provides a lot of basic information that would have been harder to access in the past.

Business letters cannot be replaced for certain purposes, however. In many cases where there is a legal issue, for instance, the business letter provides a formal way of documenting that someone has been informed of an issue. In addition, it provides a more formal way of addressing a prospective employer, which will be covered in a different chapter. Essentially, the business letter serves the role as the most formal kind of written communication.

Business letter format has been established for many years, although in recent years it has changed to become a bit more efficient. The PDP method of communicating that we have discussed in regard to memos and e-mails works very well with business letters, too.

First, let us look at the basic format of a business letter:

[Name of Your Business (if there is one)] [Your Street Address (or the address of your place of work)] [City, State, and Zip]	*Sender Address*
[Date (Month, Day, and Year)]	*Date*
[Name of Person You Are Writing (if known)] [Street Address] [City, State, and Zip]	*Inside Address*
RE: [Subject of Letter]	*Subject Line* *(optional)*
Dear [Name of Person]:	*Salutation*
The first paragraph should identify the point of writing.	POINT
The second paragraph (and the following paragraphs if necessary) explains the details related to the main point.	DETAILS
The last paragraph identifies the plan or encourages feedback.	PLAN
Sincerely, [hit enter key four times}	*Closing* *Signature space*
[Your Name] [Title (if applicable)]	*Identification*
Enclosures: [Number of Enclosures]	*Enclosures* *(optional)*

Please note that the patterns and examples provided in this text are all done in a block format. Other formats exist, such as the modified block format, which place the date and other elements of the letter away from the left margin. We recommend the block format since it is the cleanest format, it is the easiest to use, and it is probably the most common letter format in use today. In addition, note that there are no paragraph indents in block format. The letter is single spaced with blank lines in between sections and paragraphs.

Two optional sections have been included in the letter format: the subject line and the enclosures tag. These are not used in most business letters. The subject line can be useful in communication that needs to identify case numbers, work order numbers, and that sort of identifier. The enclosures tag identifies the number of enclosures if there are other documents sent with the letter.

Finally, one question that is often asked regarding letters is what to do when you are writing to a company but you do not know the name of the individual who will read the letter. In years past, a salutation reading "To Whom It May Concern:" was recommended, but though that is still acceptable, it is falling out of use. It is more common today to simply delete the salutation when you don't know the name of the recipient.

Business letters in the last century have developed from an extremely formal document to a slightly less formal and more streamlined document. Around the turn of the century, it was common to spend the entire introductory paragraph communicating positive goodwill to the recipient, as well as closing with statements such as "Your humble servant." Thankfully, today, we can use a very efficient PDP structure to get our point across efficiently and still maintain formality.

The following example shows a business letter using proper business letter format and the PDP communication pattern:

River City Electronics Repair
1215 Grassy Butte St.
Cornell, NE 69044

October 2, 2015

Robert Sherman
3433 Midland Drive
Cornell, NE 69044

RE: Customer Account #87623

Mr. Sherman:

Your account is entering four months of past due status. Please call me to arrange a payment schedule so that we may avoid a collections process.

River City Electronics values its customers and at the same time must maintain profitability to support our employees and the services we provide to the community here in Cornell. We prefer to deal with our customers directly rather than pass customer information on to collections agencies.

Due to the length of time your account has been past due, please be aware that October 30 will be the final deadline to make payment arrangements with us before we will have to pass this issue on to our collections agency.

Thank you for your attention to this matter. I can be contacted directly at (123)123-1234.

Sincerely,

Melissa Brown
Owner, River City Electronics Repair

Enclosures: 1
     Customer Invoice #32444

TOOLBOX: Mend It Before You Send It!

This chapter has discussed written communication from the very short text message through e-mails and business letters. Regardless of the form of the message, the best tip we can give is to always read communication before sending it with an eye toward correcting punctuation, spelling, and grammar. A simple spelling and grammar check if you are using electronic communication can clean up the basics. Beyond that, learn to *look at everything you write as a draft* and always review it before sending. If you are not good at grammar or spelling, find someone who is good at editing and enlist his or her help. Professional communication reflects your (and your company's) professionalism.

If you are in need of a resource to explain grammar issues or even find a format for a certain kind of a document, check the Purdue Online Writing Lab at owl.english.purdue.edu.

Finally, as you review the documents you create, always check for **PDP**: do you start off with a sentence or two that identifies the **point**, move into a body section that provides **detail** for that point, and end with a **plan** or encourage feedback?.

CHAPTER 3
THE EMPLOYMENT PROCESS

The employment process can be somewhat complex, but this chapter breaks it down into four necessary components: the cover letter, resume, follow-up letter, and interview. For some of us, this process can be intimidating because we get in the mindset that there are others applying for the same jobs who are more qualified. Keep in mind that this process is more about who can communicate his or her qualifications better than the rest of the field.

We always start a discussion about the employment process with two assumptions:

1. Most applicants submit substandard materials.
2. Most applicants fail to fully communicate their skills.

You may be shocked to hear this, but it should be encouraging news and give you an advantage. The percentage of people who simply don't follow directions in this process, or submit very weak materials, is staggering. Being careful about how you prepare for the employment process will easily put you ahead of most of your competition.

Let's think about the process of screening possible employees for a moment. Here's a flowchart of the various levels of the typical hiring process.

15

Please note that early in the process, if you are a qualified candidate, there may be little chance for being screened out, assuming you follow the directions the company provides for applying. If you take a detail-oriented approach and communicate your qualifications for the position, you should have no trouble reaching beyond the first level of screening.

One of the mistakes that people often make in the early employment process is assuming that your character matters more than your skills. Actually, the reverse is true, unless you happen to have a personal connection with an individual who is leading the hiring process. As you move further into the process, the character you project, for instance, in an interview, will begin to be more important. In the beginning, however, *it's all about the skills*.

An example: a prospective employee communicates via the cover letter and resume that he is prompt, courteous, and a very fast learner. Another competing prospective employee communicates via the cover letter that he has the required degree, experience in specific areas of the field, and mentions specific skills covered in the job description. Which employee do you think will advance in the screening?

Keep in mind that at early stages of the employment process, a human resources department with a checklist of skills may be doing the initial screening. The person who clearly communicates the skill set that the employer is seeking will win over the person who communicates their favorite personal qualities almost every time.

Therefore, the methods described in this chapter will focus each document on communicating your skills in the clearest and most professional manner possible. One final piece of advice: be detail oriented and spend some time on your materials. The sad fact is that most applicants do not. This communicates a negative message about your skills and attitude to a prospective employer. The applicant who puts together a polished, complete package will win almost every time.

COVER LETTERS

Traditionally, the cover letter accompanies the resume and provides an introduction to the applicant for the prospective employer. It should establish the basic qualifications of the applicant, as well as provide an introduction to the resume. We should note that cover letters are not always used as they are presented here in every company's application process. They are still a required part of the process for many companies, so being able to put one together is an essential skill. Creating a cover letter will also help you develop language to talk about your skills that will be useful in any application process.

The cover letter is your first chance to show your communication skills to a prospective employer. Play back the requirements listed in the description of the job. If the company asks for a basic set of qualifications (perhaps a degree, years of experience, or other specifics), make sure that your cover letter communicates that you have those qualifications. Beyond that, look at the description of the job duties and try to highlight some of the items on your resume that show your ability to perform those duties.

The cover letter should be written in proper business letter format as discussed in Chapter 2. It may be submitted via postal service, electronic mail, or in some cases via a website form or upload mechanism. Make sure that you follow the directions in the job listing to which you are responding.

The following page shows the basic structure of a good cover letter. It is immediately followed by an example job listing and a cover letter written for that specific position.

[Your Street Address]
[Your City, State, and Zip Code]

[Date]

[Name of Hiring Manager (if known)]

[Name of Company]
[Company's Street Address]
[Company's City, State, and Zip Code]

Dear Hiring Manager: [note: this salutation may be left out if you do not have a specific person you are addressing]

Paragraph 1

[Here specifically identify your purpose ("I wish to apply for…" or "Please accept my application for…") and specifically identify the position. Also identify the source of information about the job opening.

Paragraph 2

[Here is where you tell them you are qualified for the opening. You may "break the ice" by saying something positive about the company, whether it is reputation or location or another positive attribute. Don't overdo it. Move right into playing back the basic qualifications listed in the job description, along with providing a few specific examples of skills or accomplishments that relate to the job. Get the prospective employer interested in reading your resume. In some cover letters, this could extend into another paragraph.]

Paragraph 3

[In this paragraph, communicate to the prospective employer that you have enclosed your resume, application form, and any other requested documentation. At this point, you may also give them any other relevant information, such as a link online to a portfolio of your work, if that is common in your field. If this information is very straightforward and simple, you may include this information in the next or previous paragraphs.]

Paragraph 4

[In this paragraph, close with a request for an interview and indicate your willingness to be flexible in arranging the interview. This is the feedback loop discussed in Chapter 2, and one of the most important opportunities to provide for feedback throughout your lifetime will be providing contact information for a prospective employer. Be sure to include your phone number and e-mail address.]

Sincerely,

[Signature in this Space]

[Your Name]

18 Communication: Tools for Technicians

Sample job listing for an electrical apprentice (with keywords highlighted):

Sparklight Electric is seeking electrical apprentices who are ==self-motivated== and comfortable with ==solving problems==. Our company is growing fast and needs ==reliable== individuals who can work by themselves, under supervision, and as part of a ==team==.

Prospective employees will be subject to drug screening and background checks. Qualified applicants will have a valid driver's license and ==one year of field experience==.

Responsibilities include assisting journeyman electricians with various installations, ==performing work as directed== by supervisors, ==maintaining== equipment and clean work areas, making sure that parts are stocked for projects, and ==troubleshooting== electrical systems.

Required skills are strong ==communication== skills, ability to ==interpret diagrams== and electrical drawings, ability to use ==electrical formulas== to perform calculations, knowledge of the ==National Electrical Code==, and the ability to ==bend conduit== and operate ==trenching== machines.

The above job listing provides a typical listing as it would appear through a job service office, online listing such as those found at Monster.com or even a posting on a bulletin board.

It is important to remember the feedback loop in your communication on possible employment. The employer has taken time to emphasize that they need certain skills, so playing them back in a cover letter can be the first step in showing off your communication skills. On the following page is an application letter that has been carefully crafted to respond to the job listing and emphasize the skills of the applicant as they relate to the needs of the employer.

1234 Amperage Street
Voltage, OH 32132

February 14, 2016

Sparklight Electric
45 Paycheck Rd.
Welton Bay, OH 32414

Dear Mr. Ohm:

Please accept my application for the position of electrical apprentice. I found your job listing in last Friday's online edition of the Welton Bay Press.

The position appeals to me because it would allow me to remain in the region, close to family and friends. In addition, your company has a reputation for providing quality service to customers and I am confident that I have the experience, skills, and qualities to be a part of your team. My references and past supervisors will verify that I work well both independently and as part of a multi-person team in residential electrical installation work.

I meet all of the basic requirements in the job listing. I am a recent graduate of the Electrical Technology program at Voltage Technical College. For the past three years, I have worked part time and summers for an electrical contractor, and I completed an internship with Great Lakes Electric in Voltage, OH. I am knowledgeable in electrical theory, electrical math, and troubleshooting electrical problems. Conduit bending and trenching are two of the skills I have practiced for many hours on residential jobs.

I look forward to working with your company and continuing to learn as I seek my journeyman electrician's license. Please contact me at (555)555-5555 or joexample@exampletel.com to schedule an interview. I am available most afternoons and weekends. I will be glad to flex my schedule to accommodate your needs.

Sincerely,

Joe Example

RESUMES

The resume is probably the most-discussed document in the employment process, with many books and lists of rules written over the years to guide the prospective employee. Unfortunately, much of what has been written is not very useful. Keep in mind that in the early stages of the employment process, *it's all about the skills*.

This philosophy has led to the creation of the *chronological skills-core* resume. The idea of a *chronological* resume was developed decades ago, along with other resume styles such as functional resumes. For entry-level technicians, we believe the chronological resume is the best basic format. It offers an opportunity in all of its sections to offer specific, relevant information that is easy for everyone to process, whether it is the human resources associate with a checklist of skills helping screen applicants, or the hiring manager at the end of the process reviewing two finalists' application materials to make the choice of who to offer the position.

So, what is a *skills-core* resume? That is our term for a chronological resume that forms an unbroken core of education, experience, and qualifications that are all focused strongly on the skills that you can offer the prospective employer.

We didn't invent the chronological resume format, but when it is crafted as we have described below with specific detail and precision of language, it will communicate your skills better than most applicants' resumes.

The five basic sections of a chronological skills-core resume are:

Objective	This is a simple phrase that indicates your career objective, for instance, "to obtain a position as a lineman." It may also communicate your longer-term aspirations, if you wish.
Education	This section outlines each degree or diploma you hold in reverse chronological order, as well as providing basic information on the institution, location, graduation dates, and possibly even a short course listing.
Employment	This section outlines each position you have held in reverse chronological order, as well as providing basic information on the business, location, dates of employment, and a short description of the duties of each position, as well as the skills gained while performing the job duties.
Qualifications	This piece is simply a list of work-related skills or certifications.
[Optional Sections]	Any other sections that you wish to include (Awards, etc.)
References	This section should list three to four references, including names, titles, and contact information.

Note that the highlighted sections form an uninterrupted core of skills. The education section provides information on skills you have learned from institutions you have attended, the employment section provides information on skills you have demonstrated at other jobs, and the qualifications section should provide a list of any other work-related skills or certifications you hold. Between those three areas, your resume should give *a complete picture of your skill set* to a prospective employer.

With a skills-core resume that provides specific, relevant information in all sections, you will have an advantage over other prospective employees who do a poor job of communicating their skills in their application materials.

TOOLBOX: Rules for Resumes

Traditionally, there are some basic guidelines to follow when creating a resume:

1. No complete sentences. Anywhere (when have you ever heard that from an English teacher?).
2. Use reverse chronological order. List your most recent educational institutions and experiences first, and then go back in time in those sections.
3. No errors in spelling, punctuation, address format, etc.
4. Be specific and complete in the information you provide.
5. Make it visual. Use cues such as headings and bulleted lists to break up information.

On the following page is an example resume in a very simple format that does not require a template or any complicated formatting beyond tabs and spacing. You should be able to see how the skills-core resume focuses on skills throughout the middle sections. Please note that this is not the only way to format a resume. The individual sections can be formatted using other layouts. However, the overall flow of the resume and focus on skills should be in place.

Joe Example
555 12th Ave NW
Mastodon, ND 58988
(555)555-5555
joeexample@implementsrus.com

Objective:
    To become a diesel technician

Education:

North Dakota State College of Science, Wahpeton, ND — May 2015
Associate in Applied Science, Caterpillar Dealer Service Technician
    Courses: Engine Fundamentals, Transmissions, Hydraulics, Electrical, Air Conditioning, Welding

Mastodon High School, Mastodon, ND — May 2012
High School Diploma
Courses: Automotive, Metal Fabrication

Employment:

Raptor Machinery Company, Mechanicsville, ND 58989 — June 2012-current
Intern/Shop Labor
    Maintained tools and shop equipment
    Cleaned shop area

(continued)

Learned from experienced technicians	
Performed repairs on a variety of Ag equipment	
Ready Made Pizza, Mastodon, ND 58988	Summer
Assembled and cooked pizzas	2010-2011
Maintained clean workspace	

Skills:
  Licensed for forklift operation
  Certified in air conditioning
  Caterpillar technical software
  Ability to weld with oxyacetylene and arc units

References:

Robert Randall, supervisor, Raptor Machinery Co.	(555)222-2222
Greta Denton, owner, Ready Made Pizza	(555)333-3333
John Galliano, diesel instructor, NDSCS	(555)444-4444

INTERVIEWS

Interviewing is for some applicants the hardest part of the process, and for others, it is the easiest. The key to doing a good interview is displaying good communication skills throughout. You will be evaluated on your attentiveness, professionalism, and how completely you answer questions. You want to strike a balance between humility and confidence. Remember that sometimes confidence can be seen as arrogance, so speak in confident truths about your abilities, but don't inflate them.

TOOLBOX: General Rules for Interviewing

1. Dress neatly and in a manner one level above the job you will be performing.
2. Avoid negative statements about yourself or previous employers.
3. Be attentive and make eye contact with your interviewers.
4. Completely answer questions.
5. Don't be afraid to ask for questions to be repeated, especially if they have multiple parts.
6. Ask follow-up questions and show a genuine interest in the company.

Many companies have interviewing practices that involve a group of people, rather than having one supervisor interview the candidates. Be ready for a group of interviewers. Make sure that you engage each of them directly when you are answering individual questions.

To prepare for an interview, review some of the common interviewing questions that are easily found by searching online. Be ready with specific examples for how you work within teams, manage your time, and other basic issues that employers often address in the interview. Also be ready to give the interviewer(s) a quick rundown of your experience. It is helpful to bring extra copies of your resume to the interview. It will help you highlight your most significant experiences and accomplishments.

Interviewing questions can usually be organized into four major categories:

Warm-up questions (also called resume questions) are usually asked at the beginning of interviews to get the interview going and to get the applicant comfortable with talking about his or her qualifications. They are usually questions that could be answered by looking at the applicant's resume. Examples include:

- How many years have you been working in this field?
- Give me a quick run-down of the education you have received relevant to this position.
- Tell me about your work experience in this industry.

Work habits questions are usually asked toward the first half of the interview. At this point, interviewers are trying to get an idea of how you will function in the environment of the company. These questions may range from very simple questions to slightly more complex questions aimed at your preferences and comfort with working in certain situations. Examples include:

- Tell me about your experience working as a member of a team to achieve a task.
- How many times in a given week were you late at your last job?
- Do you prefer to work on your own or do you like to be surrounded by other people?
- Can you describe what kind of a supervisor you prefer?
- What kinds of things bother you from other employees at work?

Problem-solving questions often present a scenario or ask you to think through a problem or situation. These kinds of questions can challenge you, but if you don't panic and methodically work through the problem, your interviewers will appreciate your ability to think on your feet. Examples include:

- What would you do if you knew a coworker was stealing parts from inventory?
- How would you handle the situation if a customer falsely accused you of damaging his vehicle while you were performing service on it?
- When you think your supervisor is wrong about something, how do you deal with the situation?
- If you are forced to choose between completing a service call and meeting your boss for an important meeting, how would you prioritize?

Off-the-wall questions are seemingly bizarre questions that usually have some relevance to the job, but their connection is hard to see at first glance. They are not always used in interviews, but sometimes one or two is inserted into the interview to see how you deal with the unexpected. Examples include:

- If you could have superpowers, what would they be?
- What is your favorite movie character? Why?
- If you had to live on an island and could only keep two things, what would they be?

24 Communication: Tools for Technicians

In addition to interview questions, some interviews also involve competency testing or aptitude testing to determine if you or your skill level is a fit for the job. Learn as much as you can about how the interview meeting will be conducted.

Finally, be confident. If you are called for an interview, you are qualified for the job. Be prepared and ready to clearly communicate specific information about your skills and qualities.

FOLLOW-UP COMMUNICATION

Follow-up communication is not just an exercise in writing another letter or e-mail for your technical communication class. It is an essential part of the employment process, since it is a practical way to maintain contact with an employer after your materials are submitted and keep them thinking about you and your skills.

If you are looking for one good reason to write a follow-up, be aware that many job applicants simply do not follow up on communication with a prospective employer beyond submitting their resumes and cover letters.

Practically speaking, there are three reasons to follow up on your original communication:

1. You have submitted materials but not heard anything for some time from a prospective employer and you want to check on your application status.
2. You are further along in the employment process and have had your interview, and you would like to thank the interviewer(s).
3. You are formally accepting or rejecting a job offer.

For all three purposes, the message is very simple and the message will be very short. Unlike a typical business letter or cover letter, your message can probably be conveyed in one or two short paragraphs. The format of a follow-up letter is the same as any conventional business letter if it is to be mailed. If a follow-up is done via e-mail, the heading address, date, and inside address can be removed and in addition the rest of the letter format used directly within the e-mail.

Finally, a follow-up letter can be organized with the same PDP (Purpose, Details, Plan) pattern as any other short communication. The example on the next page shows a very short follow-up e-mail thanking the prospective employer for an interview.

To: bbennett@examplecompany.com

From: JoeExample@implementsrus.com

Re: Friday's interview

Date: Monday, April 17, 2016

Mr. Bennett:

Thank you for interviewing me on Friday. I greatly enjoyed my visit to your offices and shop. Your employees were a pleasure to meet and I learned a lot about how your company functions. I was especially impressed with the cleanliness and professionalism of your operation.

I am very interested in working with you in the future. If I can provide any additional information, please contact me at (555)555-5555 or joeexample@implementsrus.com.

Sincerely,

Joe Example

[end formatting]

Note: although this follow-up is formatted as an e-mail, notice the formal features of the business letter that we have added such as the greeting and using "Sincerely" at the end to mirror the complimentary close in a business letter. Those features can add an air of professionalism to a very basic memo.

CHAPTER 4
TECHNICAL DESCRIPTION AND INSTRUCTION

Communicating in many occupations includes being able to tell customers or fellow employees about the technical aspects of equipment or products. This may take the form of being able to help a customer understand how different parts of a mechanism work together, helping a coworker understand how something should look when it is assembled correctly, or instructing someone in the operation of a machine.

This chapter starts with information on providing visual support, which is very critical to both technical description and instruction. The combination of good written explanation with good visual support creates powerful communication for different audiences to be able to understand technical information.

VISUAL SUPPORT

Good visual support basically involves using images to reinforce or enhance your message. Images used within documents or presentations should be clear, easy to understand, and be focused on the message or part of the message they support. Too much visual information can sometimes distract the reader if parts of the visual are not relevant.

A good method of choosing visuals is to ask yourself the following questions:

What is the **purpose** of the visual?
Can a **connection** be established with the information in the document?
Does the visual have the exact **information** it needs to fulfill its purpose?

If there is a clear purpose for the visual to be included, a connection is easily established to the written information, and there is a level of information in the visual appropriate to the part of the message it supports, then it should be included. The logistical aspects of including the visual can then be addressed.

> **TOOLBOX: Inserting Visuals into Your Document**
>
> Proper **placement** involves locating the visual in the document in such a way that it is adjacent to (or at the very least connected to) the information it supports.
>
> **Captioning** involves giving the visual a name, such as "Figure 1," along with a short description, such as "Cordless Drill."
>
> **Referencing** the visual is making sure that the visual is called out in the text that it supports. You might use a reference such as "See Figure 1" or build the reference into a phrase within a sentence, such as "The cordless drill, as shown in Figure 1, is a power tool used for boring holes in various materials."
>
> For examples of visuals used within documents, see the example technical description or the example instructions in the following sections.

TECHNICAL DESCRIPTION AND THE VISUAL SENSE

Describing things in technical terms involves being very aware of the visual sense, as well as issues such as the purpose or function of parts, how they fit or relate to one another, and even how they are fastened or joined.

The visual sense allows human beings to process information very quickly in terms of form, size, texture, color, and position. This set of features can be broken down into an acronym: FaSTCaP. Any visual description, whether the author is a poet or a technician, relies on those five areas. Let's discuss each of the five areas in a little bit more detail:

Form

Form at its most basic level involves being able to describe the shape of something. Generally, we can use words that describe specific geometric shapes, such as rectangular and oval. However, not all mechanical objects are found to be in perfect geometric shapes, so sometimes we have to get creative. Making comparisons to things that human beings routinely encounter is one way to effectively describe things. For instance, you might describe something as "shaped like a camel's hump" to describe how it appears on the back of another part.

Size

With size, we can once again leverage words that give us specific ways to discuss measurement. One of the earliest activities in school is learning units of measurement such as feet and inches. However, it is sometimes hard for people to imagine units of measurement outside their experience. This can be seen on the golf course—some players are good at judging distances in yards, while others mightily struggle! For someone who is not a machinist, thinking in terms of thousands of an inch might be difficult. As with form, we can make comparisons to help our audience understand. We might, for instance, communicate a measurement of 0.003 inches. To help someone understand that measurement more effectively, we might compare that measurement to the thickness of a sheet of paper.

Texture

Texture is not always as straightforward as form and size in terms of its description. At first, it may seem that it does not fit into the visual sense, as it relates more to the sense of touch. However, keep in mind that texture can also be seen and visualized due to the existence of visual clues, such as the reflection of light and shadow. We can see that an object is smooth, for example, because we have touched other objects that reflect light in the same way.

Description of texture can also be more complex. First, specific words related to texture can be used. Beyond simplistic descriptions of rough and smooth, we have words for how metal and wood can be finished in many industries. For instance, those familiar with manufacturing metal products might discuss bead-blasted finishes, polishing metal parts to a certain level to increase performance, or even discuss the rough-cast nature of certain parts. Second, we can make comparisons to the textures of commonly known objects. A well-known tool manufacturer, for instance, compares its screwdriver handles to the texture of a cat's tongue. Creativity can be very effective when we do not have a specific word for the job!

Color

Color as an element of the visual sense can be difficult to communicate if we oversimplify it. Think of the many times that you hear someone describe the color of his or her car to a gas station attendant. "It's the red one" would be a common statement. But is it just red? Obviously, the human eye can visualize hundreds of thousands of shades of red, assuming that colorblindness is not an issue. Therefore, we can usually do better than describing only the colors we find in an eight-crayon box. Think of describing things in terms of the biggest box of crayons imaginable. Crayola, for instance, has a color called "macaroni and cheese." It is a perfect rendition of the color of that common food that almost all children ask their parents to make. Within the name of the color is a direct comparison. Another example might be the phrase "school bus yellow." The second we utter it, most of us can identify the color in our minds because of the direct comparison to something we see almost every day.

Color is also an area that merits a warning about using specific color names. Usually, specific language is very desirable, but an interior designer may know a word for a color such as "mauve," while the next person may have never heard that term. Identifying the shade of colors, and perhaps using comparisons will solve the problem of certain sets of individuals using specific color words. And lest you think that interior designers are the only workers concerned with color, keep in mind that a welder watches for certain colors in metal to appear, and those working with electronics are often faced with a wiring harness that rivals the number of colors in a deluxe crayon box.

Position

Last, but not the least in importance, position involves describing where things are at with regard to space or the other things around them. As with form and size, we can use mathematical or scientific words to describe position. We might describe something as perpendicular or parallel to another part, for instance. Once again, though, we might need to get a little bit more creative with our language to describe how things fit together. For instance, we often make reference to parts of the human body, describing objects as "fingers" and "feet." Making a comparison directly to something people can visualize is just as effective with position as it is with size and shape.

Along with placement, position involves describing how parts are fastened or joined together. The example of a dovetail joint in woodworking or a description of the type and grade of fasteners used in joining a tractor fender to the body shows that there are a great variety of issues involved in describing mechanical objects assembled with various parts.

Notice the pattern that emerges as all of these elements of the visual sense are discussed. Each can be described in very technical terms according to scientific or mathematical qualities, as well as described by using comparisons to common things to help audiences understand. The combination of effective, specific scientific or mathematical language, along with helping people relate to things they already know, provides a high level of accurate description.

Any good technical description also addresses the function of parts. This does not always mean a lengthy discussion of how a mechanism works (sometimes that is saved for creating instructions). It does mean perhaps identifying the purpose of a part, explaining how that part functions with other adjacent parts, and at times how parts are fastened within their assemblies.

An example would be explaining the intake manifold on a common car engine. The purpose of an intake manifold is to pass the fuel or air mixture in between the fuel delivery system (most commonly fuel injection), which sits directly above it, and the cylinders of the engine below. A good technical description would identify that purpose, as well as how the intake manifold relates to the fuel delivery system and the cylinder heads of the engine. Combined with a good visual description, we can help our audience truly be able to visualize what we are trying to communicate.

As we address writing a formal technical description document, you should be able to see how the FaSTCaP method of visual description combines with the purpose, function, and assembly of parts to provide a very effective and efficient way to clearly represent mechanical objects to any audience.

WRITING A TECHNICAL DESCRIPTION

Please note that although we are presented with a formal technical description document pattern in this chapter, it is far more likely that you will practice this skill in your future career in a number of ways that do not include a formal document. Your technical description skill will be used in conversations with other technicians, communication related to troubleshooting problems, discussing proper assembly of parts, questions for manufacturers related to mechanisms, and many other ways of discussing technical aspects of machines. The document described here provides a way of practicing all of the aspects of technical description in an integrated way that fits into this course.

Building upon the PDP (Point, Details, Plan) method of communicating discussed in Chapter 2, we can build a larger document with the same three-part construction. We will simply expand the initial section into a bit more complicated introduction, build the details of the document in the body using a more complex method, and provide a conclusion that sums up the document.

A map for building a technical description might look like this:

Introduction

Defines the object, gives its purpose, gives a quick visual overview, and lists the main parts. An image supporting the description is usually included in this section, unless the supporting image is too big and is offered on a separate full page of the document.

Body

Breaks down into a description of each part underneath a heading. This is the section where the FaSTCap Method of description is used most heavily. Each part should be described in visual terms, as well as its function and how it relates to other parts.

Conclusion

Provides a short conclusion to cap off the document. A very effective way to conclude is to tell who uses the object or where it is used, as well as perhaps repeating its purpose.

On the following page is an example of a technical description. Note how the visual support and each written section work together to provide a very good picture of the parts of a mechanism.

EXAMPLE

Front-drag Spinning Reel

A front-drag spinning reel is a hand-operated mechanical device that is placed on a rod. The combination of a rod and reel allows for casting and retrieving baits to catch fish.

The spinning reel shown in Figure 1 is a typical reel of its type. Most spinning reels have the same type of parts and are similar in operation. The body of the reel is usually a composite plastic or metal alloy, with parts mostly made up of either plastics or metal alloys. The average spinning reel weighs under a pound.

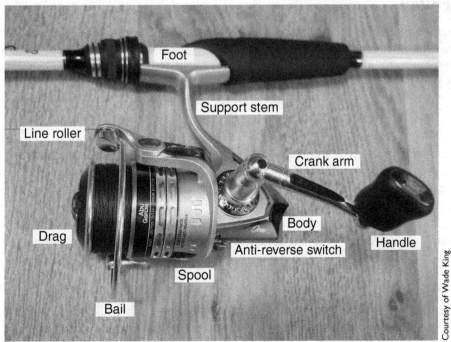

Figure 1 Parts of a front-drag spinning reel.

Spinning reels vary in size with the most typical models measuring approximately six inches long, three inches wide, and four inches high. They come in a wide variety of colors and finishes. A spinning reel has a foot that attaches to the rod, with the rest of the assembly forming a fixed spool in front to hold the fishing line, a bail for releasing and capturing line, and a crank and handle for retrieving the line. The rest of the parts are listed in the diagram and in the following descriptions.

Drag

The drag allows the user to place a desired amount of tension on the line, from allowing it to be pulled very easily from the spool to making it almost impossible to pull line from the spool. This is useful for allowing caught fish to surge and run without breaking the line. On the front of the reel, the drag is a circular knob with a flat raised piece across the middle allowing it to be easily manipulated. Usually about an inch and a half in diameter, the drag knob is usually made of a composite or metal alloy.

Spool

Fishing line is stored on the spool, and as the bail turns around the fixed spool, it wraps the line in a consistent pattern. The spool, located directly behind the drag, is cylindrical and has a lip on the front and a skirt on the back to keep the line from falling off. Spools can be either plastic or metal alloy. Many current spinning reels come with a spool for monofilament line and a shallower spool with a grippy, rubber surface in the middle for braided line. Spools are often marked with the line capacity of the reel.

Line roller

The line roller allows the line to flow smoothly onto the spool. It is located at the end of the wire that forms the bail, since that is the place where the line catches when the bail is engaged. It is a small, cylindrical piece about ¼" in diameter that rotates freely. Usually, it is made of metal that is highly polished so that the line does not snag.

Bail

The bail is a piece of relatively thick wire that is formed in a horseshoe shape and attached to a carrier that spins around the spool. The bail can be flipped forward to release line for casting, and when the reel is engaged or the user flips it backward, it allows line to be gathered onto the spool by cranking the reel. The bail is the defining part of a spinning reel. It spins around the fixed spool, rather than operating like a winch, as with a baitcasting reel. Depending on the quality level of the reel, the bail can be made of titanium or other metal. It is always polished or plated for smooth operation.

Body

The body is essentially a casing that holds the other parts together, allowing them to be mounted and work together. Mostly watertight, it protects the internal bearings, gears, and shaft. Located in the midst of the external parts, it is usually rectangular in shape. It may be made of carbon fiber in a very expensive reel, or more commonly an aluminum alloy or composite plastic. On the average, the body of a spinning reel is approximately two and a half inches long by about one and a half inches high. Finishes can vary widely, including paint, plating, anodizing, or polishing.

Gears

The gears are internal to the reel and are not shown in Figure 1. They work together to transfer motion and multiply the force from the crank to turning the bail around the shaft and spool of the reel. About the size of a nickel or dime, they are circular with a hole in the middle and teeth on the outside edges that engage with each other. They are precision-machined and polished for smooth operation.

Bearings

The bearings, internal parts not shown in Figure 1, allow the crank and shaft to turn smoothly. They take the form of very small spheres held in a circular casing or tiny rods held in a cylindrical casing. They vary in size according to the size of the shaft they support. The quality of a spinning reel sometimes depends on the number of bearings and the level of polish and fitting involved. Generally, when more bearings are specified on the reel, it will operate more smoothly than a reel with fewer bearings. Typical spinning reels have from three to ten bearings.

Anti-reverse switch

The anti-reverse switch allows the reel to be set to anti-reverse, a mode in which the reel cannot spin backward, or to allow the reel to be cranked in either direction to retrieve or let out line. It is a small, rectangular tab about a half-inch wide that is usually located on the bottom of the reel body directly behind the spool. It is usually made of plastic, but sometimes will be formed from a metal. It is serrated or textured so that it can be gripped with a finger.

Foot

The reel foot, connected to the reel assembly by a stem on the top rear of the reel, allows the reel to be attached to a rod. Most rods have a reel seat with a locking collar that mates with the reel foot. Rectangular in shape and approximately two and a half inches long, the reel foot is molded or cast to have a curved top to conform to the rod. The texture often matches the body and stem of the reel.

Support stem

The support stem connects the reel foot to the rest of the reel and allows the reel to hang below the rod at a distance that allows the bail to spin clear of the rod. Generally, it drops for about an inch below the reel foot in a straight line, and then angles back to meet the rear of the reel. The shape varies depending on how it is formed or cast. Usually, the support stem is approximately ½" to ¾" inch in diameter. The support stem is sometimes cast or molded along with the body, and with some reels it is attached to the reel body with screws or pins.

Crank arm

The crank arm of the reel, which on most reels can be attached for left or right-handed users, extends from the rear of the reel where it crosses the body of the reel and engages the gears. It is held on by a slender threaded bolt from the opposite side and bends forward to about the midpoint of the reel where the reel handle is attached. The shape can vary depending on the manufacturer, and it is usually about 1/2″ in diameter.

Handle

The reel handle is attached at the end of the crank arm to allow the user to place it between finger and thumb and crank line onto the reel. It is often a ¾″ long flat piece of aluminum or plastic covered in a soft rubber with textured dots to allow for gripping it effectively; although on some reels it can be a cylindrical wood piece. It swivels on the end of the crank arm to allow for front or backward reeling.

Spinning reels are used by a variety of people for fishing for a myriad of fish species from shore, boats, and piers in both fresh and salt water. They are generally inexpensive and make good stream fishing rods because of their ability to cast long distances and retrieve line quickly. They can be used for a variety of fishing techniques including jigging, rigging, and fishing with floats.

INSTRUCTION

Communicating clear instruction, or telling someone how to do something, is a vital skill for the workplace. It relies on technical description, since being able to break down something into parts and their characteristics is necessary for explaining how something should be assembled or operated.

At work, instruction can come in various forms. It could be verbally explaining a procedure to a new employee, creating an instruction manual for a product, or explaining to a customer how to operate a piece of machinery. Whether the form is verbal or written, the same pattern of communication can apply.

Since we have already been through an in-depth discussion of description, we can simplify instruction to a very basic pattern and a small set of rules and have most of the guidance we need.

The pattern of instruction, whether it is oral or written, generally should include the following elements:

Introduction

We also call this section the overview, because it generally should provide an overview of the process. If you think about any situation where you learned something new, you probably know that the most effective teachers are the ones that look at the big picture first. What are you trying to accomplish? Why does it need to be done? How long does it take? What tools or materials are necessary? These are all issues that should be covered before you start breaking down the steps of a process.

A checklist for the introduction follows:

- Identify the goal and purpose
- Tell about any conditions that need to be in place
- Communicate a tools or materials list
- Identify the length of time the process takes
- Give a quick overview of where the process starts and ends

This method maximizes efficiency. How many times have you spent more time wandering around looking for tools than you did on performing a simple repair? A good introduction prepares the reader for the tasks laid out in the step-by-step instructions.

Finally, some processes require specialized equipment or materials that may have safety considerations. Safety warnings can be communicated in the introduction, especially if the safety issue occurs throughout the overall process. They can also be inserted along with an individual step if that is the only instance the safety issue is relevant.

Body

The body of a set of instructions essentially lays out the steps, along with any visuals that are necessary to support any of the steps.

The first issue in writing steps is how to structure them. Is the procedure you are describing to someone a very simple "Point A" to "Point B" chronological set of steps? Another possibility might include the procedure having a series of operations that make up the overall procedure. Operations are sets of sub-steps that make up smaller procedures.

Making the choice of how to structure your steps is usually fairly easy. If you can break the procedure down into several overall parts, you will need to use operations with sub-steps. If you can lay down a series of steps with a clear beginning and ending that all relate to the same goal, you will not need to use sub-steps and you can use a simple, linear structure.

An example of organizing a procedure in a linear structure would be writing a set of 23 steps for tying a fly for fishing. That is a process that starts with a bare hook and ends with a complete lure. The steps in between all build upon one another.

An example of organizing a set of instructions with sub-steps might be inspecting a combine for field work. One might have a series of operations including checking all of the lights, checking the hydraulics, checking fluids, checking tires, etc. that includes a set of sub-steps for each of those operations. Further on in the chapter, there is an example provided for each method.

Finally, the rules for writing steps are simple:

1. One action per step
2. Number and sequence the steps in a logical manner

Since we have already described the structure in some detail, numbering and sequencing steps is a very simple task. However, what does "one action per step" mean? If your audience has never performed a procedure before, you might have to remind yourself to keep the process simple. In describing how to change a tire, for instance, you might start with a step of pulling off the road to a safe spot. Then you might advise your reader to check their owner's manual for the location of the jack. If you overwhelm someone who is new to a process with multiple tasks in one step, you can lose them in the details. A simple command like "jack up the car" is actually not so simple. It can become frustrating if someone does not receive clear communication of the steps that are implied. A quick test is to look for the verbs you have included in each step. One action verb per step will usually indicate that you have reduced a step to its most simple form.

Finally, remember in writing steps to include visuals where you think they will help the most, as well as helpful advice or cautions to avoid problems that may occur throughout the procedure. In addition, remember to caption any visuals and make reference to them to connect them to the written information.

Conclusion

The conclusion of a set of instructions could be as simple as a stop sign symbol, a bit of commentary along with a photo of a completed project, or a paragraph that indicates the current procedure is finished and the next steps if your instructions are part of a larger manual or set of procedures.

SUPPLEMENTAL INFORMATION IN INSTRUCTION

Finally, instructions often need supplemental information inserted within the steps in order to help the end user accomplish the task. Notes, tips, cautions, and warnings all fall into the category of supplemental information that might help the audience understand the process or task better.

Typically, this type of information is handled by inserting it in a visually prominent way so that the user can pause and perhaps gain important information before making a mistake or causing the task to be performed incorrectly.

Cautions and warnings are the most critical types of insertions and can occur anywhere within a set of instructions. If an entire set of instructions is describing how to use a dangerous piece of equipment, that information should be prominently shared before the steps even begin. On the other hand, if one step is the only point in the process where the dangerous equipment is used, it makes sense to include the warning immediately before the step. An example might look like this:

WARNING: Soldering irons and molten solder can cause extreme burns to the user. Follow safety precautions listed on equipment and avoid contact between the soldering iron and skin or other objects that can be destroyed by heat.

Sometimes, cautions aren't necessarily related to safety issues, but may be simply an identification of what to avoid:

CAUTION: Do not overtighten screws that are threaded into wood. The hole can become stripped and the fastener will not hold.

Or, in some cases, we just want to give additional information that might help someone successfully complete a task:

TIP: Several different adhesives can be used to attach the plastic trim, but we have found that a waterproof construction adhesive applied with a caulking gun is the best method.

Color, borders, or a shaded box will all call attention to something you want the reader to see before moving to the next step or section in the instructions.

On the following pages is a set of instructions written with operations and sub-steps. Reviewing it should reinforce the concepts in this chapter and give you a pattern to use in the creation of your own instructions. Remember when writing instructions that depending on the purpose, it may make sense to have a very linear process of steps from beginning to end, or it may make sense to use a series of operations and sub-steps, as previously discussed in the chapter.

EXAMPLE

How to Prepare and Rig a New Fishing Kayak

Buying a new fishing kayak is exciting and the urge to take it out on the water is great, but some careful preparation can make sure that your first experience on the water is a good one. Kayak fishing is an activity that combines two relatively sophisticated activities. Being a good kayaker means being safe and prepared, and good fishing relies on a fair amount of preparation and organization, as well.

Rigging and preparing your new fishing kayak will take approximately one afternoon if you have the tools and materials ready. You will want to work in an area with good light with the kayak supported well. The process will start with putting together safety equipment and move through installing several essential and nonessential items. The process will end with a focus on storage for your fishing gear (or perhaps where to put your lunch).

Tools Required

#2 Phillips screwdriver
Small adjustable wrench
Lighter
Cordless drill
1/4" drill bit

Materials and Necessary Items

Personal flotation device (PFD)
Air horn (optional)
1/4" rope, 35 feet
Carabiners (2)
Anchor trolley kit including:
    -rope
    -plastic ring
    -cleat
    -2 small surface mount pulleys
Mighty mounts or gear tracks (as many as desired)
Rod holders (number and type as desired)
Bolts, washers, and nuts for rod holders (1/4" stainless steel)
Seadek or similar adhesive foam padding
Kayak crate or cooler (according to preference)

Step 1. Assemble safety equipment.

- Choose a personal flotation device. Many options are available, but you will want one that offers good range of movement and is intended for paddlesports (see Figure 1).

Figure 2 A typical paddlesports PFD.

- Always keep the PFD with your kayak so that when you leave for the water, it is not left behind. Even in relatively shallow, calm water a person is only one mistake away from drowning.
- Have a first aid kit on board. Fishing involves sharp hooks, knives, and sometimes fish with teeth.
- Consider other safety equipment depending on your purpose and unique situation. This may include an air horn and signaling mirror if you are paddling large expanses of open water or a knife for quickly cutting anchor lines if you are fishing in rivers. Think carefully about what you will need.

Step 2. Set up a bow line. Every fishing kayak should have a bow line on board even if it is rarely used, as it provides a length of emergency rope as well as a way of tying your kayak to objects or towing your kayak.

- Cut a 20′ length of 1/4″ rope.
- Melt both ends of the rope with a lighter to prevent fraying.
- Using a simple noose knot, tie a carabiner to one end, or both ends if preferred (see Figure 2). Visit animatedknots.com for details on tying a noose knot.
- The bow line will be used for pulling your kayak behind you through shallows, tying it off to tree branches, and it can either function as the anchor line or provide a spare anchor line.

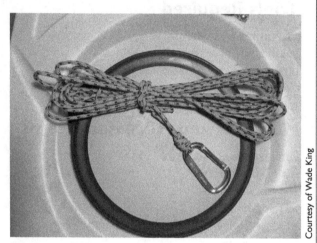

Figure 3 A completed bow line.

Step 3. Rig an anchor trolley.

This is optional, but if you ever want to fish in a fixed position you will need to have a method of anchoring. A trolley system is the safest and most adjustable way to set up an anchor.

WARNING: Anchoring in current requires some experience and careful planning. Keep a knife handy so that the anchor line can be cut. If it becomes caught, your kayak can be submerged by fast current quickly.

- Carefully choose the front and back locations for the anchor trolley pulleys. They will control the range of where you can place your anchor, so if you want to use it from bow to stern, place them as near to the bow and stern as possible. If you do not want the range of control all along the boat, you can place the pulleys further toward the middle of the boat.

- Before drilling holes for each of the pulleys, make sure that you can access the hull in both locations from the inside so that the hardware can be installed.
- Drill a 1/4" hole in each of the pulley locations you have chosen.
- Attach each pulley to the kayak with the bolt provided passing through the pulley and the plastic of the kayak. Behind the plastic of the hull, next place a washer and then a lock nut. All hardware should be stainless steel.

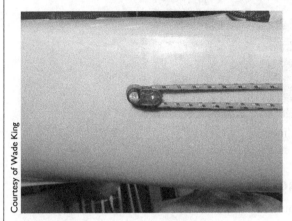

Figure 4 Orientation of pulley.   **Figure 5** A typical trolley system.

- Orient each pulley so that the round part is pointing to the middle of the kayak and tighten the nuts (see Figure 3).
- Cut a length of 1/4" rope to a length equal to twice the distance between the pulleys plus an allowance of four feet for tying knots.
- Pass the rope through the front and rear pulleys so that there is a continuous length across the top between the pulleys, and the two ends can meet on the bottom (see Figure 4).
- Using a noose knot, tie each end of the rope to a plastic ring (triangular in our example), and make sure as you tie the last knot that the rope is tight around the pulleys. You may also include a quick snap as shown in Figure 4 if you want to be able to release the line.
- At this point you can check the assembly and try to move the top of the rope back and forth with your hand. It should cause the metal ring on the bottom to move back and forth. This will become your attachment point for the anchor line.
- Install a cleat in line with the top of the anchor trolley rope at a location that is reachable from the seat of your kayak (see Figure 5). This will allow you to hold the rope in one place so that the anchor point doesn't move. Use stainless steel bolts with a washer and a lock nut on the back side of the hull. Make sure you check so that you can access the location for installing the nut before you drill holes for this installation.

Figure 6 Cleat in trolley line.

Step 4. Install rod and accessory holders.

Even if you are not going to troll with your rods, you will want a secure place to be able to put them down when you have to tend to other business.

- Carefully decide on the location of rod holders or any other accessories you want to install on the kayak. Mighty Mounts and Gear Tracks both provide a versatile mounting point that will accept multiple accessories. Figures 6 and 7 show possible mounting locations for both methods. Figures 8 and 9 show mounted accessories.

Figure 7 A four-inch Gear Track.

Figure 8 A Mighty Mount.

- Install all mounts with the provided or recommended hardware. Mighty Mounts are typically bolted to the kayak with 1/4″ bolts, and a washer and locknut or a backing plate with threaded holes on the back side. Gear Tracks are typically installed with self-tapping screws. Consult the manufacturer's installation recommendations.

CAUTION: When installing all mounts, remember to check for access inside the kayak's hull to install the backing hardware.

Figure 9 A Scotty rodholder mount.

Figure 10 A RAM rodholder in Gear Track.

Step 5. Add noise-reducing foam.

Part of fishing is not spooking the fish, so it may be necessary to reduce any rattles or rubbing between parts that you can identify.

- Look for areas that are likely to squeak or rattle. The most common point to find these problems are where seats mount to the deck.
- Cut a small piece of Seadek or similar adhesive-backed foam product and place it underneath the offending item so that it cushions it from the kayak.

Step 6. Optimize storage with a crate or a cooler.

Most fishing kayaks have a "tank well" named for the area scuba divers would carry their tanks on a kayak. Behind the seat, it is a storage area usually criss-crossed with bungee (see Figure 10).

- Decide whether you would like to install a crate to carry fishing rods and tackle (see Figure 9), or a cooler for your lunch and beverages.
- Depending on what you are placing behind the seat, you may have to reconfigure how the bungee criss-crosses the area and possibly use carabiners or hooks to tie the crate or cooler down to the kayak. Make sure that you secure whatever you choose to carry on your kayak. One possible crate configuration is shown in Figure 11.

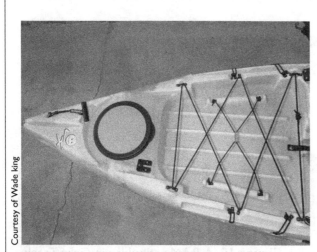
Figure 11 Tank well area of fishing kayak.

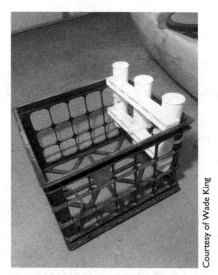
Figure 12 Homemade kayak crate.

Now that you have your brand new fishing kayak rigged, you can enjoy your careful preparations on the water and catch more fish! For more information on kayak rigging, YouTube has dozens of videos that are just one search away.

CHAPTER 5
REPORTING INFORMATION

Often, the idea of writing a report scares people. It brings to mind images of demanding teachers and requirements of notecards, outlines, and piles of source material. At work, the idea of writing a report can include some of those elements, but often, reporting is actually the simple process of telling someone something.

This chapter breaks down reporting into informal and formal reports. An informal report might be a simple e-mail notifying your boss of a problem that requires a solution. A formal report could include doing research, for instance, on types of forklifts and reporting recommendations to a supervisor on which forklift would work best in a warehouse situation.

Typically, informal reports are transmitted by simple methods such as memos and e-mail messages, while formal reports are formatted in a much more official manner with a cover page, sections with headings, and supporting documentation.

Summary is an important skill to practice in relation to reporting information, since it gives you the ability to condense information and relay it to someone else. This is particularly useful in the instances in which you might be asked to gather information and share it with others. Being able to quickly research a topic, boil information down to main points, and clearly present it to others will make you a valuable communicator in your place of work.

SUMMARIZING INFORMATION

Being able to take a pile of information and boil it down to what is relevant to your situation or workplace is a very valuable communication skill. At some point in your career, someone will likely ask you to gather information and pass it on to someone else.

Summary involves both putting something into your own words, as well as reducing the amount of information to about twenty percent of the original work. Summary is not the same as paraphrasing, which is just rewording the original without reducing it.

The key to summary involves finding the main points of the original work. In many trade magazines, journal articles, and company reports, it is easy to find the basic pieces because headings are used to break up the information. Summary does not have to be difficult if you focus on the original structure of the document and follow it. The second level of finding the main points of a written work is identifying the topic sentences in each paragraph, which are most often conveniently found at the beginning of a paragraph.

Although you will rarely have to write a formal summary in the workplace, you will have to incorporate summary into reports and presentations. However, the following is an example summary of a magazine article. Note the main idea of the article is identified in bold. A good summary always mentions the author and the main idea at the beginning and then provides a complete and organized breakdown of the original work's main points.

In addition, note that this formal summary begins with a citation identifying the article and its source.

EXAMPLE

ARTICLE SUMMARY

Oldham, Scott. "Hot Pursuit: Riding Shotgun with the California Highway Patrol." Popular Mechanics January 1997, 62–67.

In this article on the California Highway Patrol, Oldham focuses on two officers and their vehicles: Mark Garrett and his 5.0L Mustang, and Charles Gilliland, who drives a 350 Chevy Caprice. He rides with both men, evaluating their work environment and the vehicles they use to perform routine patrol and traffic safety duties.

Oldham begins his article by describing the dangerous environment the officers work in. Roll call begins with a survival creed that reads in part "Don't let them kill you on some dirty freeway." The author puts on a bulletproof vest and begins two days of riding with patrol officers.

First, Oldham rides with Mark Garrett, an officer who prefers the 5.0L Mustang for patrol duties. His preference is made clear by his choice of personal cars, a Vortec supercharged 5.0L Mustang. The author experiences traffic stops, accident responses, and routine patrol with Officer Garrett, who drives the Mustang hard, from cruising speed to 110 miles per hour. The only shortcoming to the Mustang in the author's view is that it is lightweight and cramped. Otherwise, the speed and reliability of the engine seem to make it perfect for traffic safety duties.

Next, the author rides with Officer Gilliland, who performs many of the same patrol duties with a Chevy Caprice police cruiser. The advantage of the heavier Caprice is shown when Gilliland pushes a wrecked BMW off the road with the pushbar on the front of the car.

Scott Oldham ends his days of working with the highway patrol by pulling off his bulletproof vest, thankful that he doesn't have to wear it again.

Overall, the article provides a clear look at a specialized area of law enforcement: highway patrol. It gives a clear technical description of the most important equipment the officers use—their cars. For anyone who has ever wondered about what really lurks under the hood of those black and whites, it answers a lot of questions.

Now that we have had a chance to address the foundational skill of summarizing information, we can work on patterns of communication that work well for reporting information. The Toolbox section that follows identifies a method that builds on the PDP method of short communication that we have previously discussed in the text. It gives you a way to think about organizing information that is easy to remember and follows natural patterns of thinking to create an effective message.

TOOLBOX: The Past, Present, Future Method

Organizing reports is simple if you think in terms of the past, present, and future:
PAST: What happened?

PRESENT: What is the current status?

FUTURE: What are you going to do or ask others to do about the situation?

Most instances of informal and formal reporting can be approached using this method. For any situation describing a problem and solution, it can be particularly effective.

If you combine the past, present, and future with the basic idea of the Point, Details, Plan (PDP) method of communication described in Chapter 2, a plan for writing a report might look like this:

SUMMARY STATEMENT: Called the "Point" in our PDP method, the first short paragraph of your report should identify the problem or the main point being addressed, and could quickly summarize the past, present, and future elements.

PAST: In this section, you can identify the background of the situation at hand or give the history leading up to the present. Think of this as "telling the story."

PRESENT: This section should identify what is happening "now." The present situation should be clearly outlined. What are the problems, challenges, or areas that need to be addressed? What is the current status of your work? This is often the area of a report where research or statistics are presented if they are relevant.

FUTURE: Finally, the last section or conclusion of your report should look ahead and identify actions that need to be taken. What still needs to be done? What will you do or what are you asking others to do?

INFORMAL REPORTS

As mentioned previously, informal reports can be formatted in a number of ways. Usually, an informal report will make use of a short form of communication, such as those discussed in Chapter 2. Reporting information to someone internally in your company is most likely to take the form of an e-mail or memo.

It should also be noted that in areas where technicians prepare reports using an electronic system, such as that found in automotive, truck, and implement repair facilities, the Past, Present, Future method also works very well.

The best way to illustrate the Past, Present, Future model flow of information in an informal report is to provide the example shown. It is an e-mail from an employee to his supervisor explaining a vehicle accident.

EXAMPLE

> To: Jenna Wilhelm, residential installations supervisor
> From: Duane Mariotti
> Re: Vehicle incident
> Date: 5/27/2015
>
> Yesterday morning, I was involved in a traffic accident in Carson City, NV with our Ford service truck (#PH3227, license AZ 2147 RT). No injuries occurred in the accident, but the service truck was damaged in the front end and will need repairs before it is drivable. I will need a temporary replacement truck while mine is being serviced to complete our work on the Croydon Springs Healthcare Campus.
>
> While driving south on the 800 block of Shelby Boulevard, I observed a black sedan approaching the intersection of 7th Street quickly from the right hand side. I slowed, but unfortunately did not have time to avoid the accident, as the sedan passed through the stop sign and struck the right front of my vehicle. The momentum spun my service truck around and it ended up with the front end on the curb on the opposite side of the street. I quickly shut the vehicle off and checked the other car to make sure that the occupants were not injured. The driver indicated to me that he was distracted by his passenger for a moment and missed the stop sign.
>
> I immediately dialed 911 to report the accident and a Carson City police officer arrived within about five minutes and recorded insurance information from the other driver and from me. I reported to the officer the details of the accident, and he told me that a police report will be on file and available as of tomorrow, May 28. I emphasized to him that the other driver appeared to be at fault due to running the stop sign.
>
> After taking care of business with the police, I checked for any damage to tools and equipment besides the truck. There was none, so I removed my essentials from the service truck, locked all

of the toolboxes, and waited for the tow truck driver to arrive. The truck is now located at Primo Towing and Salvage in Carson City. I took a cab to my room at the Camden Inn on Horseshoe Drive West, where I am currently working to plan the continuation of my project.

I called the number on our insurance card to report the accident, but would you please follow up and see if there is anything else that they need? Also, I will need you to request a replacement fleet vehicle or rental to be sent here so I can transfer tools and equipment. There is a Ford service truck similar to the one assigned to me available on our lot since we finished the project in Tulsa.

Assuming we can replace the service truck within two days, I believe we can stay on schedule with our project. I have notified my Croydon Springs contact that I cannot make the meeting today, but will meet with him in the morning to plan the initial phase of installation and assure them we will be able to continue work after this setback.

Please reply to this e-mail or call me at (987)654-3211 when you have made arrangements, and in the meantime I will continue whatever work I can complete.

Note how the previous example follows the Summary Statement, Past, Present, Future flow of information. The first paragraph is a quick summary of what happened (Past), how it's affecting the employee (Present), and what needs to be done (Future). The second and third paragraphs tell the story, providing relevant details (Past). The fourth paragraph transitions into the current status (Present), while the last two paragraphs look ahead (Future) and request action from the supervisor to solve the problem and move on with the project.

With this easy-to-remember pattern, you can quickly put together an informal report on just about any situation. You can easily use the basic structure to produce an incident report, project status report, inspection report, document a repair, or relay to a coworker or supervisor essential information to solve a problem.

FORMAL REPORTS

The main differences between an informal and a formal report are in the way they are formatted, the audience, and sometimes the amount of research necessary. Longer reports can require more than one level of headings, and usually involve a much more formal structure including a cover page, table of contents, and a list of references.

A sample template for a formal report appears on the following pages. See each of the sections for explanations and for an example of including visual support.

EXAMPLE

Title of Report

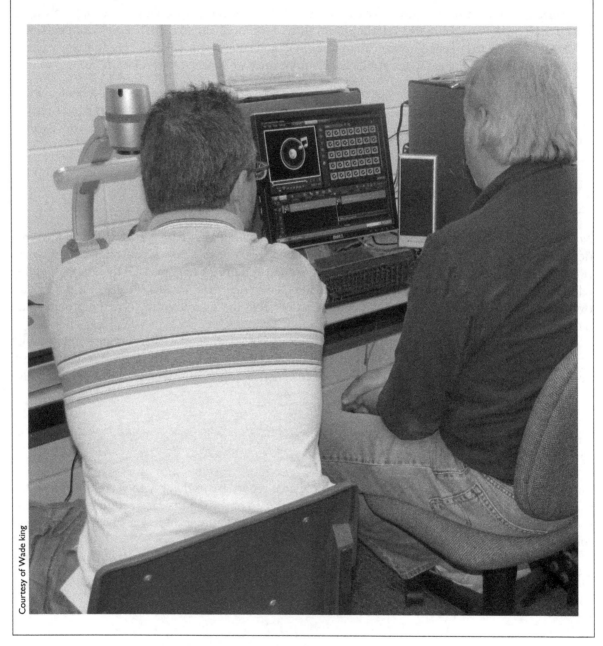

Courtesy of Wade king

Your Name

Department or Division Name
Company Name
Date

Title of Report

Your Name

Department or Division Name
Company Name
Date

SUMMARY

In a formal report, this statement should summarize the objective of the work, the history of the project or problem, the work or research done, and examine results or look ahead to next steps. As with the informal report, the summary statement should cover the main points of the past, present, and future elements.

TABLE OF CONTENTS

Introduction/Background

First-Level Heading .... Page #

    Second-Level Heading .... Page #

    [repeat for however many headings exist]

First-Level Heading .... Page #

    Second-Level Heading .... Page #

    [repeat for however many headings exist]

First-Level Heading .... Page #

    Second-Level Heading .... Page #

    [repeat for however many headings exist]

Conclusion/Results/Next Steps .... Page #

Appendix/Supporting Documents .... Page #

References .... Page #

INTRODUCTION

This section may be titled something besides "introduction" such as "Background on the Adelaide River Dam Project." It should provide context for the work being described in the report and give the reader any information necessary to understand the work or research being described in the report.

Note that paragraphs are formatted in block style (no indents), with a double space separating each paragraph. In the following sections, two levels of headings will be demonstrated, as well as how to format visuals with captions and references.

FIRST-LEVEL HEADING

The next heading should begin the sections of the main body of the report. It may begin the past, present, and future flow of information previously discussed. This is where the story of the work or the research begins. The heading should describe the overall content of the section in a few words.

The heading text should be formatted in text two point sizes larger than the basic text of the report. In this report, the basic text is 12 point and the introduction and first-level headings are 14 point. Once again, paragraphs are formatted in block style.

Second-Level Heading

For breaking up information within large sections further, second-level headings may be used. They should be boldfaced in the same size as the basic text of the report (in this case 12 point).

Second-Level Heading

Second level heading should only be used when there is more than one topic to break down into subsections.

FIRST-LEVEL HEADING

Within sections of the report, it will be necessary to place elements that may include diagrams, photos, or charts. All visual items should be referenced in the text to tie them to the material of the report, as well as captioned with a short description.

In the text of the report, references can be made via a direct reference in a sentence such as "Figure 1 shows one of the support piers for the building." References can also be accomplished by using an introductory phrase, such as "As shown in Figure 1, . . ." Finally, a parenthetical reference could also be used at the end of a sentence (see Figure 1).

The caption of the visual element should be formatted as in the example below, in a slightly smaller point size than the basic text (11 pt in this example) and use a short phrase after the identification of the figure number. The phrase should identify the content of the visual element and its relevance to the information in the report.

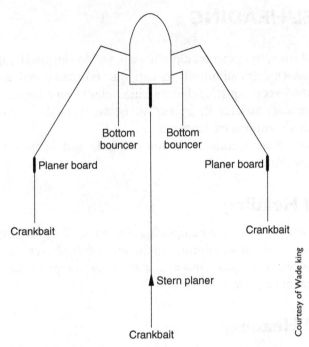

Figure 1 A diagram of a typical trolling spread with five lines.

If a table or a chart is used within the report, captioning and referencing those visual elements are done in the same manner.

Second-Level Heading

For the rest of the body text in this report template, we will use the Latin "filler text" just to show the formatting of the paragraphs. Skip to the end of the report to see information on the conclusion, appendices, and references.

Lorem ipsum dolor sit amet, consectetur adipiscing elit, sed do eiusmod tempor incididunt ut labore et dolore magna aliqua. Ut enim ad minim veniam, quis nostrud exercitation ullamco laboris nisi ut aliquip ex ea commodo consequat. Duis aute irure dolor in reprehenderit in voluptate velit esse cillum dolore eu fugiat nulla pariatur. Excepteur sint occaecat cupidatat non proident, sunt in culpa qui officia deserunt mollit anim id est laborum.

Second-Level Heading

Lorem ipsum dolor sit amet, consectetur adipiscing elit, sed do eiusmod tempor incididunt ut labore et dolore magna aliqua. Ut enim ad minim veniam, quis nostrud exercitation ullamco laboris nisi ut aliquip ex ea commodo consequat. Duis aute irure dolor in reprehenderit in voluptate velit esse cillum dolore eu fugiat nulla pariatur. Excepteur sint occaecat cupidatat non proident, sunt in culpa qui officia deserunt mollit anim id est laborum.

FIRST-LEVEL HEADING

Lorem ipsum dolor sit amet, consectetur adipiscing elit, sed do eiusmod tempor incididunt ut labore et dolore magna aliqua. Ut enim ad minim veniam, quis nostrud exercitation ullamco laboris nisi ut aliquip ex ea commodo consequat. Duis aute irure dolor in reprehenderit in voluptate velit esse cillum dolore eu fugiat nulla pariatur. Excepteur sint occaecat cupidatat non proident, sunt in culpa qui officia deserunt mollit anim id est laborum.

   Lorem ipsum dolor sit amet, consectetur adipiscing elit, sed do eiusmod tempor incididunt ut labore et dolore magna aliqua.

Second-Level Heading

Lorem ipsum dolor sit amet, consectetur adipiscing elit, sed do eiusmod tempor incididunt ut labore et dolore magna aliqua. Ut enim ad minim veniam, quis nostrud exercitation ullamco laboris nisi ut aliquip ex ea commodo consequat. Duis aute irure dolor in reprehenderit in voluptate velit esse cillum dolore eu fugiat nulla pariatur.

Second-Level Heading

Lorem ipsum dolor sit amet, consectetur adipiscing elit, sed do eiusmod tempor incididunt ut labore et dolore magna aliqua. Ut enim ad minim veniam, quis nostrud exercitation ullamco laboris nisi ut aliquip ex ea commodo consequat. Duis aute irure dolor in reprehenderit in voluptate velit esse cillum dolore eu fugiat nulla pariatur.

CONCLUSION

In this section, summarize the work completed and put it into context. Are there next steps that need to be completed? If the report is based on research, summarize the findings and include any final recommendations that need to be made.

APPENDIX A: TITLE OF APPENDIX

An appendix to the report might be more detailed data, information from another source that explains something mentioned in the report, or a chart that supports a point made in the report. Appendix titles should begin after a page break and appear in the table of contents. The general method of titling appendices is to use letters.

Include as many appendices as necessary, but keep in mind that your reader may not need every piece of information you reviewed in building your report. Only include relevant information.

APPENDIX B: TITLE OF APPENDIX

Lorem ipsum dolor sit amet, consectetur adipiscing elit, sed do eiusmod tempor incididunt ut labore et dolore magna aliqua. Ut enim ad minim veniam, quis nostrud exercitation ullamco laboris nisi ut aliquip ex ea commodo consequat. Duis aute irure dolor in reprehenderit in voluptate velit esse cillum dolore eu fugiat nulla pariatur.

REFERENCES

The final page of the report should be a list of references you have used (assuming there is research in the report). Generally, American Psychological Association (APA) format is a good method to use if you need to build a list of sources but have not learned a format that is appropriate for your field. The Purdue Online Writing Lab at owl.english.purdue.edu is a good quick reference for APA and Modern Language Association formatting of reference pages.

Each entry should follow the general pattern of providing the author (with last name first), title of the article or memo in quotes, name of the publication if relevant, date, and page numbers. List each article or publication in alphabetical order.

Hopefully, this chapter has given you a series of patterns to use when you need to report information. Whether it is a formal or informal situation, information needs to be passed among employees of a company for the company to function well. Using the summary statement, past, present, and future flow of information will almost always work as an organizational method. If the reporting situation requires more formality, the formal report format can be used to apply the structure necessary to get the job done.

Finally, we recommend practicing the skill of summary for the workplace. Being able to pass information in a condensed and meaningful form to coworkers, along with other communication skills, is a skill that leads to leadership opportunities. Efficient and effective communication never has to be more complicated than the situation requires.

CHAPTER 6
ORAL COMMUNICATION

This chapter will focus mostly on presentations—whether they are formal or informal, delivered to groups outside of your company or delivered to coworkers. Chapter 2 discussed short forms of communication, including voicemail and quick verbal communication. The Point, Details, Plan (PDP) method of communication is a very quick way to organize those short forms of communication, and an expanded method of that form works well for delivering presentations.

Many of the same patterns that work well for organizing written documents work well for organizing formal oral presentations or speeches, as well. In many cases, your oral presentations at work will be delivering information that you have already reported in written format. Rather than focusing on the organization of presentations, we will primarily discuss strategies for effective oral communication.

INFORMAL PRESENTATIONS TO COWORKERS

Much of oral communication in the workplace is conversational, and it serves a great purpose. The quick back-and-forth communication that happens throughout the day helps get the job done, as essential information is shared, questions are asked and answered, and important yes or no issues can be solved quickly. At times, however, there will be a need for a more formalized sharing of information that involves sharing a concept or a plan with coworkers, bosses, or perhaps individuals you supervise.

In those situations, it helps to have in mind the areas where people commonly fail to express themselves effectively.

TOOLBOX: Talking to the Team—Common Problems in Oral Communication

The most common problem areas in oral communication and presentation are speed, eye contact, and feedback.

Many people **speak too fast**, especially when they are nervous. Remember to relax, slow down, and speak deliberately. It's easy to be in a rush to "get it over with" if you don't enjoy public speaking, but if you move through information too fast, your coworkers won't enjoy the experience at all.

A lot of individuals **don't make enough eye contact** when speaking to groups of people. Sometimes this is a confidence issue, and sometimes it is an issue of wanting to hurry the process along. Making eye contact ensures that your audience is engaged and allows you to gauge their level of understanding and interest.

Quite often, speakers in both formal and informal settings **don't provide opportunity for feedback**. Think of the many times you may have complained that someone "doesn't listen." Part of presenting information is making sure that your audience understands the information. If you don't get feedback, it is hard to know if that level of understanding has been achieved.

Keep in mind that although you may be in a situation where you are communicating with coworkers who you know very well, you don't want to be so comfortable that you forget to prepare your information beforehand, organize your information well using PDP or Past, Present, Future methods, and try to engage the audience.

FORMAL PRESENTATIONS

With formal presentations, there is usually more at stake. You are representing your company to people who may not be familiar with you or your company. More attention to detail is necessary and preparation is the key.

Preparation not only means having your material ready and "doing your homework" but also means getting a mindset together so that you are confident, relaxed, and open to questions or feedback. If you are meeting with a set group of people, try to find out a little bit about them or their company culture. In addition, prepare beforehand to make sure that you have enough supporting material or handouts for the number of people in the room, make sure that you know how to use any equipment that you will have to use for your presentation, and confirm the location of your presentation so that there are no last-minute glitches that will cause you to be uneasy.

STRATEGIES TO ENGAGE YOUR AUDIENCE

As mentioned, knowing the background and culture of your audience contributes greatly to helping them understand your material. In addition to presenting relevant information, engaging your audience can be a challenge if you haven't done very much public speaking.

Engaging your audience means more than keeping them awake. Showing enthusiasm through the entire presentation from beginning to end will give them a positive charge. You may feel yourself losing momentum and energy, but keep the excitement going! Begin your presentation with a question or a big idea that gets your audience thinking. As you move through your presentation, make sure that you keep your audience engaged by making eye contact and asking them questions directly, involving them in the discussion, or providing visuals or examples that vividly punctuate the ideas you are presenting.

Most people attending a presentation from outside your company will want to know the answer to the question "What's in it for me?" so remember to consistently tie the content of your presentation to their company's interests, their needs, or their preferences. You may be trying to partner with another company on a project, sell a room full of people on an idea, or change the attitude of your community or school board. No matter what your purpose is, the audience need to know why they are listening to your speech in that room.

Finally, show your audience that you value them by providing them a chance for feedback. Ask them at the end if they have any questions or further comments. Invite them to contact you with any future questions.

Many presentations in today's industrial and corporate environments make use of technology to help display relevant supporting visuals. Using the following guidelines will help you to put together a successful digital presentation:

GUIDELINES FOR USING DIGITAL PRESENTATION METHODS

1. Use as little text as possible on your slides and use a 20 point or larger font size.
2. Focus the slides mostly on key phrases and visuals and verbally fill in the specific information.
3. When using charts or visuals, simplify them to the message you want them to carry.
4. Avoid using a large variety of transitions and backgrounds in favor of consistency.
5. Keep in mind that the first and last slides will be the most memorable, so make them count.
6. Do not read directly from the projection screen or computer screen. Remember to maintain eye contact with your audience.

Many of the issues involved with informal and formal oral presentations go back to the basics discussed in Chapter 1. Your presentations need a clear purpose, you must know your audience, and you must always remember to encourage feedback so that your presentation is more than a one-way communication.

A FINAL NOTE

Remember, the patterns discussed in this book work equally well for both oral and written communications. If you practice the PDP and Past, Present, Future methods of organizing your communication, you can focus on detailed, accurate content in all of your communication and effectively share and transfer the information that is necessary to get the job done. Good communication means good productivity for you and your organization. We wish you the best of luck as you communicate throughout your career!

CPSIA information can be obtained
at www.ICGtesting.com
Printed in the USA
LVHW060017051219
639493LV00001B/2/P